AMAZING SNAKES!

KING COBRAS

BY DAVY SWEAZEY

WITHDRAWN

BELLWETHER MEDIA • MINNEAPOLIS, MN

EPIC BOOKS are no ordinary books. They burst with intense action, high-speed heroics, and shadows of the unknown. Are you ready for an Epic adventure?

This edition first published in 2014 by Bellwether Media, Inc.

No part of this publication may be reproduced in whole or in part without written permission of the publisher. For information regarding permission, write to Bellwether Media, Inc., Attention: Permissions Department, 5357 Penn Avenue South, Minneapolis, MN 55419.

Library of Congress Cataloging-in-Publication Data

Sweazey, Davy, author.
  King Cobras / by Davy Sweazey.
      pages cm. – (Epic. Amazing Snakes!)
  Summary: "Engaging images accompany information about king cobras. The combination of high-interest subject matter and light text is intended for students in grades 2 through 7"– Provided by publisher.
  Audience: Ages 7-12
  Includes bibliographical references and index.
  ISBN 978-1-62617-094-0 (hardcover : alk. paper)
  1. King cobra–Juvenile literature. I. Title.
  QL666.O64S944 2014
  597.96'42–dc23
                    2013036464

TABLE OF CONTENTS

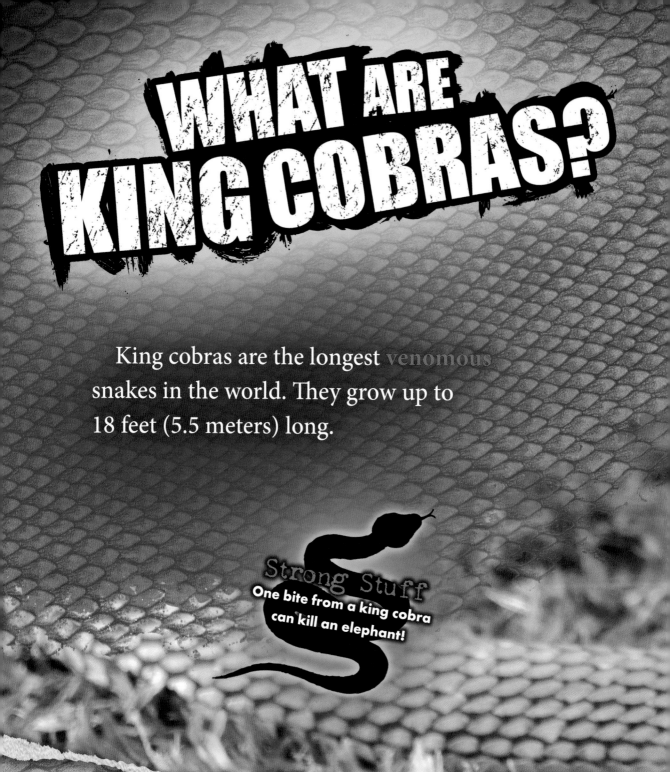

WHAT ARE KING COBRAS?

King cobras are the longest venomous snakes in the world. They grow up to 18 feet (5.5 meters) long.

Strong Stuff
One bite from a king cobra can kill an elephant!

WHERE KING COBRAS LIVE

N
W E
S

king cobra range =

Most king cobras live in the rain forests of south and southeast Asia. Many have green, brown, or black scales. Their throats are often yellow. These colors camouflage them.

King cobras are found on land, in trees, and in water. They like to stay near streams and swamps. Scutes help them slither.

A Royal Welcome

King cobras are the only snakes that make nests for their eggs. Parents protect their nest until the eggs hatch.

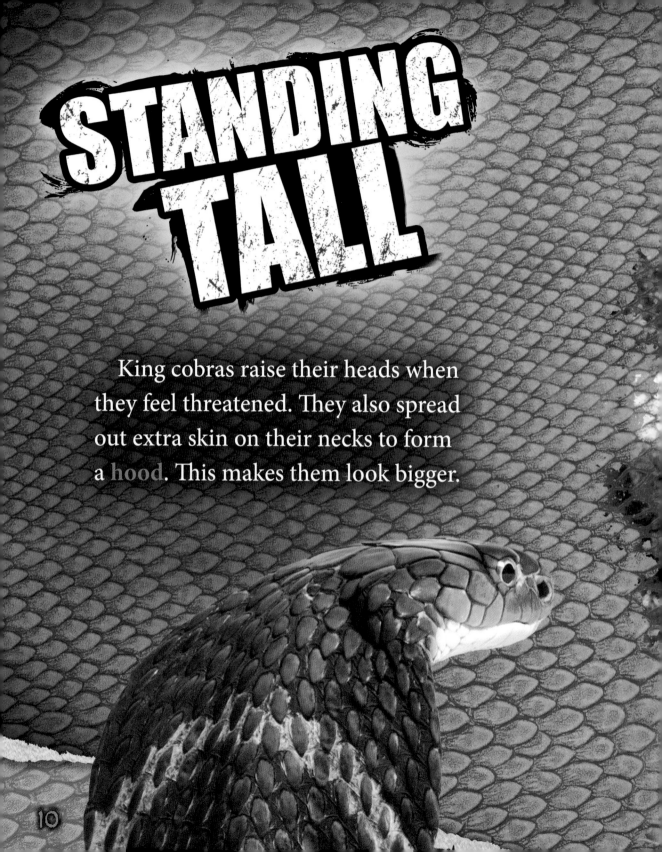

STANDING TALL

King cobras raise their heads when they feel threatened. They also spread out extra skin on their necks to form a hood. This makes them look bigger.

Heads Up

King cobras can lift up to a third
of their body off the ground.
A 15-foot (4.6-meter) king cobra
can stand up to 5 feet
(1.5 meters) tall!

11

A Hissy Fit

King cobras hiss when they feel threatened. A king cobra's hiss sounds like a dog's growl!

Stretched hoods warn predators to stay away. Brave mongooses ignore the warning. They attack king cobras.

HUNTING FOR PREY

Snake Eat Snake

The king cobra's scientific name, Ophiophagus, means "snake eater" in Greek.

King
Cobra
Prey

King cobras are active hunters. Their forked tongues help them smell snakes, lizards, and other prey.

15

King cobras bite animals with their fangs. Venom flows through the special teeth to kill the prey.

King cobras open wide with their flexible jaws. Then they swallow their prey whole!

SPECIES PROFILE

SCIENTIFIC NAME:	*OPHIOPHAGUS HANNAH*
NICKNAME:	HAMADRYAD
AVERAGE SIZE:	10-16.5 FEET (3-5 METERS)
HABITATS:	RAIN FORESTS, FORESTS NEAR WATER
COUNTRIES:	BANGLADESH, BRUNEI, CAMBODIA, CHINA, INDIA, INDONESIA, LAOS, MALAYSIA, MYANMAR, NEPAL, PHILIPPINES, SINGAPORE, THAILAND, VIETNAM
VENOMOUS:	YES
HUNTING METHOD:	INJECTS VENOM WITH FANGS
COMMON PREY:	KRAITS AND OTHER COBRAS, LIZARDS

GLOSSARY

camouflage—to hide an animal or thing by helping it blend in with the surroundings

fangs—sharp, hollow teeth; venom flows through fangs and into a bite.

flexible—able to stretch

hood—the skin that spreads around a cobra's head and neck; cobras use hoods to scare their attackers.

predators—animals that hunt other animals for food

prey—animals that are hunted by other animals for food

rain forests—hot, rainy areas with tall trees

scales—small plates of skin that cover and protect a snake's body

scutes—large, rough scales on the stomach of a snake

venom—a poison created by a snake; snakes use venom to hurt or kill other animals.

venomous—able to create venom in their bodies; king cobras release venom through their fangs.

TO LEARN MORE

At the Library

Gray, Leon. *King Cobra: The World's Longest Venomous Snake*. New York, N.Y.: Bearport Publishing, 2013.

Owings, Lisa. *The King Cobra*. Minneapolis, Minn.: Bellwether Media, 2012.

Woodward, John. *Everything You Need to Know About Snakes: And Other Scaly Reptiles*. New York, N.Y.: DK Pub., 2013.

On the Web

Learning more about king cobras is as easy as 1, 2, 3.

1. Go to www.factsurfer.com.

2. Enter "king cobras" into the search box.

3. Click the "Surf" button and you will see a list of related Web sites.

With factsurfer.com, finding more information is just a click away.

INDEX